Advanced
Newborn Care Specialist Training
Second Edition

Tonya Sakowicz

CONTENTS

This is the essential workbook to accompany your Advanced Newborn Care Specialist training. In the workbook, you will find all the information that corresponds directly with what you are learning and it allows you plenty of room to take extensive notes to ensure you are learning through visually experiencing the material, hearing it and writing down your personal notes on it. Page by page, you will have all the information you need to learn well and retain that knowledge. Students who take the Advanced Newborn Care Specialist training say this book was essential to their learning process.

Infant Brain Development

TONYA SAKOWICZ
NEWBORN CARE SOLUTIONS

Infant Brain Development

Notice these major ideas in this segment:

- In the first 3 months, what prepares them best for the future?
- What calms the brain and allows it to take in the new world when it doesn't have to "worry"
- What can we do as caregivers that helps? The 5 "S's"
- The five truths of brain development
- The 3 main Elements that meet babies' needs and give them the optimal opportunity

Infant Brain Development

- Every parent and caregiver wants what is best
- Babies are amazing—neuroscience is starting to truly study them
- For so many years, we didn't have a clue
- Until the 1960's—studies started at Kindergarten or later
- 1960's, early intervention and Head Start
- And in recent years, we are learning it starts so much sooner

NOTES:

Infant Brain Development (con't)

- ▷ Approx 1 billion brain cells at birth
- ▷ Increases 20 fold during the first month of life
- ▷ Over 1 TRILLION lines of communication by 4 weeks of age
- ▷ A healthy, nurtured and active brain means better emotional and academic development later

NOTES:

_____

_____

_____

_____

Infant Brain Development (con't)

- Do we start with videos?
- Foreign language study?
- What really works?
  - Loving Care by a consistent caregiver
  - Proper Sleep
  - Proper Nutrition
  - Proper Interaction and Engagement

NOTES:

_____

_____

_____

_____

_____

Infant Brain Development (con't)

▷ In the first 3 months, what prepares them best for the future?

▷ Mimicking the womb

▷ Brain recognizes this and transitions to life outside the womb better

NOTES:

Infant Brain Development (con't)

- Calms the brain and allows it to take in the new world when it doesn't have to "worry"
  - Nourishment
  - Maintaining body temperature
  - Comfort
  - Movement
  - Security

NOTES:

_____

_____

_____

_____

_____

Infant Brain Development (con't)

> What can we do as caregivers that helps? The 5 "S's"
>> Swaddle
>> Sway
>> Shush
>> Side hold
>> Suck

NOTES:

_____

_____

_____

_____

_____

Infant Brain Development (con't)

The five truths of brain development

The First Truth: Intelligence is both genetic and able to be influenced

- Genetic component is a huge factor
- It is not a "fixed" component
- IQ is both what a child is born with plus what happens after they are born
- Outside factors affect a child's intelligence and FUTURE generations
- It's passed on through gene development and operation

NOTES:

_____

_____

_____

_____

Infant Brain Development (con't)

The five truths of brain development

The First Truth: Intelligence is both genetic and able to be influenced

- ▷ Consistent early experiences turn on or protect against genetic traits that are already present

- ▷ Bonding matters, particularly early on, especially in negative behaviors:

- ▷ Aggression, hyperactivity and compulsivity

- ▷ These traits, once turned on, are passed on to the next generation through activated genes

NOTES:

Infant Brain Development (con't)

The five truths of brain development

The Second Truth: Most major organs are fully formed in miniature at birth except the brain

- ▷ Trivia: What one part of the body is the same size at birth and death?
- ▷ The brain is ¼ its full adult size at birth
- ▷ Brain cells (neurons) are formed before birth
- ▷ Connections between the brain cells (synapses) are formed mostly after birth
- ▷ Some send information (axons) and some bring it in (dendrites)

NOTES:

_____

_____

_____

_____

Infant Brain Development (con't)

The five truths of brain development

The Second Truth: Most major organs are fully formed in miniature at birth except the brain

- Most brain growth in the first year are dendrites
- We are taking in information way more than we are sending it out as babies and small children
- Every waking hour, new connections are made
- Brains grow and evolve (change) in response to experiences and environment
- Unique in every single individual, even identical twins

NOTES:

_____

_____

_____

_____

_____

Infant Brain Development (con't)

The five truths of brain development

The Third Truth: Our brains are born unfinished for a reason

▷ We cannot be pre-wired to meet every life scenario

▷ We grow connections as needed

▷ This is how we stay alive

▷ The speed of growth is unfathomable

NOTES:

_____

_____

_____

_____

Infant Brain Development (con't)

The five truths of brain development

The Third Truth: Our brains are born unfinished for a reason

▷ When we stop using or needing connections, they wither away (neural pruning)

▷ Those we use more strengthen and work better and faster, developing a fat layer (myelin)

▷ Growth is rapid in infancy and early childhood, peaks and are pruned significantly by adolescence

▷ For babies: Repetition, routine and reinforcement equal strong connections

NOTES:

_____

_____

_____

_____

Infant Brain Development (con't)

The five truths of brain development

The Fourth Truth: Early Development Matters

▷ The earliest connections provide the map and influence all future development

▷ Prior to birth, the "unconscious" develops—those things which happen without conscious thought

▷ Blood pressure, heart rate and body temperature

▷ These pathways are strong and stay consistent throughout life

▷ Emotional processing connections are also some of the earliest

NOTES:

Infant Brain Development (con't)

The five truths of brain development

The Fourth Truth: Early Development Matters

- ▷ Our ability to respond emotionally is formed much earlier than ever thought
- ▷ Strong connection because of the early formation
- ▷ More resistant to change
- ▷ If we create positive experiences for babies, they are more likely to grow up emotionally healthy
- ▷ We do this with: Interesting experiences, strong sense of security, lots of touch (especially skin to skin), speak to them lovingly, vary what they see and hear

NOTES:

_____

_____

_____

_____

Infant Brain Development (con't)

The five truths of brain development

The Fifth Truth: The overall pattern matters more than each small decision

- We all mess up
- Individual events don't cause long-term damage
- The overall pattern of love, stimulation and security matters more
- It's never too late to help
- The brain has the remarkable ability, with consistent repetitive improvement, to reorganize itself (neuroplasticity)
- The older we get, the longer it takes, but it is not impossible

NOTES:

Infant Brain Development (con't)

The 3 main Elements that meet these needs and give babies the optimal opportunity

First Element: Meeting their nutritional needs

▶ The brains greatest task is survival. And babies come straight from the womb with this instinct to meet their immediate and ongoing nutritional needs

▶ The Breast Crawl

NOTES:

_____

_____

_____

_____

Infant Brain Development (con't)

The 3 main Elements that meet these needs and give babies the optimal opportunity

First Element: Meeting their nutritional needs

- Babies can find the breast and latch on very soon after birth
- Found through olfactory cues from glands on the breast
- First time mothers have more of these glands
- Except in rare cases (galactosemia), breastmilk is the ideal food
- From the point of brain development, quality matters, not just calories

NOTES:

Infant Brain Development (con't)

The 3 main Elements that meet these needs and give babies the optimal opportunity

First Element: Meeting their nutritional needs

▷ It's important to recognize abnormal reactions also

▷ David's Story

NOTES:

_____

_____

_____

_____

_____

Infant Brain Development (con't)

The 3 main Elements that meet these needs and give babies the optimal opportunity

First Element: Meeting their nutritional needs

▶ What does this mean for you?

▶ You need to know about human milk: from the client and from donor sources

▶ You need to know about formulas and what they contain (the good and the bad)

▶ You need to know about alternatives

▶ You need to know why prenatal vitamins matter, even after birth

NOTES:

_____

_____

_____

_____

Infant Brain Development (con't)

The 3 main Elements that meet these needs and give babies the optimal opportunity

The Second Element: Attention and Environment

- We set up babies environments with two goals: to stimulate or to soothe/rest
- We unconsciously link attention and alertness with intelligence, and with good reason
- Environment has a direct impact on brain development and attention span
- Positive environment equals a relaxed, alert brain that takes in and responds positively

NOTES:

Infant Brain Development (con't)

The 3 main Elements that meet these needs and give babies the optimal opportunity

The Second Element: Attention and Environment

▷ What matters:

  ▷ Spending time in face to face with a trusted caregiver

  ▷ Being exposed to age appropriate play activities

  ▷ Limiting the amount and quality of screen exposure

  ▷ Down time, every day

NOTES:

_____

_____

_____

_____

Infant Brain Development (con't)

The 3 main Elements that meet these needs and give babies the optimal opportunity

The Second Element: Attention and Environment

- Paying attention requires more than one segment of the brain
- Requires coordination of the senses in several areas of the brain
- Must be alert and turn towards the object of interest
- Mental and physical shift away from what you are doing
- Maintain Focus on the new thing
- Shut out other distractions

NOTES:

Infant Brain Development (con't)

The 3 main Elements that meet these needs and give babies the optimal opportunity

The Second Element: Attention and Environment

- Babies are born alert
- Babies are instinctually drawn to the familiar, especially parent's voices
- Brazelton's example
- The first year is critical
- The perfect time for caregivers to make a conscious effort for positive impact

NOTES:

Infant Brain Development (con't)

The 3 main Elements that meet these needs and give babies the optimal opportunity

The Second Element: Attention and Environment

- Sustaining attention takes longer
- Ability to learn to shut things out takes more time for the brain to learn
- Shutting out and delayed gratification is critical for future success
- The Marshmallow example

NOTES:

Infant Brain Development (con't)

The 3 main Elements that meet these needs and give babies the optimal opportunity

The Second Element: Attention and Environment

- What can we as caregivers do?
  - No tech zone for you and parents
  - Take things back to the basics and limit or eliminate tech toys
  - Keep contrast in mind (black and white, loud and quiet, large and small)

NOTES:

Infant Brain Development (con't)

▷ Specific actions caregivers can take:

Infant: 0-6 Months
Deliberately attend to infant with frequent face-to-face time, bringing face within ten to twelve inches when speaking, using exaggerated facial expressions and mouth movements.
Make direct eye contact with infant, trying to stimulate and maintain infant's eye contact.
Use rattle or other object for tracking across the midline, re-engaging infant's eye contact continuously on the object.
Point out objects while labeling objects and actions throughout the day.
Speak to infant using *parentese* to engage infant's auditory attention.

Chart Credit: *Bright from the Start*, page 47, Jill Stamm, PhD

NOTES:

_____

_____

_____

_____

_____

Infant Brain Development (con't)

▷ Specific actions caregivers can take:

Infant: 0-6 Months

Note times of day when infant is awake and alert. Use those times for deliberate interactions.

Change/rotate toys or bright objects periodically for novelty.

Use objects and toys with high contrast colors (red, yellow, black and white) and high contrast patterns, such as stripes or checks, to attract infant's attention. Gradually add other strong colors such as blue and green.

Place mobiles and toys ten to twelve inches from infant's face.

Make faces at the infant and watch her imitate (e.g., sticking out your tongue).

Chart Credit: *Bright from the Start,* page 47, Jill Stamm, PhD

NOTES:

Infant Brain Development (con't)

The 3 main Elements that meet these needs and give babies the optimal opportunity

And the Final Element: Sleep

- ▷ This is predominantly why an NCS is hired
- ▷ Sleep has two stages: REM and non-REM
- ▷ Both are important, but adults and infants are different
- ▷ Adults: 20% REM, Infants: 50% REM

NOTES:

_____

_____

_____

_____

Infant Brain Development (con't)

The 3 main Elements that meet these needs and give babies the optimal opportunity

And the Final Element: Sleep

- Sleep deprivation in Rats:
    - Normal life span: 3 years
    - Deprived of REM: 5 weeks
    - Deprived of all sleep: 3 weeks

NOTES:

Infant Brain Development (con't)

The 3 main Elements that meet these needs and give babies the optimal opportunity

And the Final Element: Sleep

- ▷ REM is "restorative sleep"
- ▷ Dream time
- ▷ One of the 3 deep sleep stages (there are 5 total)
- ▷ Adults have 75-90 minute cycles
- ▷ Infants have 30-45 minute cycles once their circadian rhythm has developed

NOTES:

_____

_____

_____

_____

Infant Brain Development (con't)

The 3 main Elements that meet these needs and give babies the optimal opportunity

And the Final Element: Sleep

▷ The deep restorative sleep (3, 4 and REM) appear to be most critical to brain function

▷ Sleep deprivation makes us cranky and it makes babies cranky too!

▷ Impairs our ability to focus and concentrate

▷ Impairs infant ability to shift focus and concentrate

▷ Believed to lead to attention problems later in life

NOTES:

Infant Brain Development (con't)

The 3 main Elements that meet these needs and give babies the optimal opportunity

And the Final Element: Sleep

▷ Sleep impacts neuron and neuron pathway development

▷ Deep sleep allows rest and restoration

▷ Without it, the connections are not strong and malfunction

▷ Different connections are formed during sleep time than awake time

▷ Both are necessary, as is the pruning that occurs during deep sleep

▷ This is why infants spend more time in REM

NOTES:

_____

_____

_____

_____

Infant Brain Development (con't)

The 3 main Elements that meet these needs and give babies the optimal opportunity

And the Final Element: Sleep

- Lack of proper deep sleep leads to:
    - Heart disease
    - High blood pressure
    - Work and traffic accidents
    - Depression
    - Obesity
    - Auto-immune disorders

NOTES:

Infant Brain Development (con't)

The 3 main Elements that meet these needs and give babies the optimal opportunity

And the Final Element: Sleep

▷ What does that mean for the us?

▷ Knowing why infant sleep is critical and how it impacts brain development helps us know the "why"

▷ It helps us educate parents about good sleep habits for their babies

▷ It helps support why "aunt Mary" needs to stay out of the nursery

▷ Infant brains and how the develop are amazing things—we can make a difference for the future!

NOTES:

_____

_____

_____

_____

Better Business Practices

TONYA SAKOWICZ
NEWBORN CARE SOLUTIONS

NEWBORN CARE SOLUTIONS

Better Business Practices

Notice these major ideas in this segment:

- Get professional help when you need it!
- Invest in yourself
- Get a professional website, Linked-in account, Twitter, Instagram
- Get a Mentor; someone you really trust

Better Business Practices

▷ Introduction Video: https://www.youtube.com/watch?v=jottDMuLesU

▷ The world is changing, rapidly

▷ Online based contact is the way to go, but you have to do it right in order to have it noticed

▷ Where is mom in the middle of the night?

NOTES:

_____

_____

_____

_____

_____

Get professional help when you need it!

- Now is not the time to "learn" how to build a website unless you are already technically savvy or you have the time to really dedicate to it and the ability to support yourself in the mean time
- Get a professional email
- Get a professional headshot done

NEWBORN
CARE SOLUTIONS

NOTES:

NEWBORN
CARE SOLUTIONS

Invest in yourself

- ▸ Training and Mentoring
- ▸ Good haircut/style
- ▸ Get at least one nice interview outfit; preferably something neutral and easily interchangeable

NOTES:

Get a professional website, Linked-in account, Twitter, Instagram

➤ When you don't know how to do it, get someone who does!

➤ Your time is valuable—spend it on things you are really good at, improving those skills and let other people do what they are good at

➤ Don't go cheap

NOTES:

_____

_____

_____

_____

_____

Get a professional website, Linked-in account, Twitter, Instagram (con't)

When it comes to your website, for maximum connectivity, it needs to:

- Problem solve
- Mobile enabled
- Google Plus account
- Strong SEO words (include baby nurse and babynurse)
- Use video on your site, but upload it to you tube and link it (Lynn)
- Offer bits of free information through Tips (Alexandra Latten) or Blogs or ebooks
- Have a smooth, professional look that reflects you
- Have a way to capture email addresses

NOTES:

_____

_____

_____

_____

Our clients are professionals, no matter how cute their babies are

- ▷ You and your marketing materials need to be professional
- ▷ No A, B, C's and handprints
- ▷ Babies are fine if they are hi-quality shots
- ▷ Team up with a Pro in your area

NOTES:

Our clients are professionals, no matter how cute their babies are (con't)

- ▷ Can't afford a logo design pro? Fiverr! 99 Designs! Logo Contest! Elance!
- ▷ Can't afford a brochure? Evaluate if you really need one? Where do you market?
- ▷ Can't afford a business card designer?
- ▷ Can you afford NOT to have one?
- ▷ Remember: This is an investment in YOU. You will get a return.

NOTES:

NOTES:

_____

_____

_____

_____

_____

Get a Mentor; someone you really trust

- You can join our online student community and have access to our team of mentors
- You can approach someone you respect and admire, but make sure they share your values/style
- You can even hire a NCS specific business coach if you really want to take a "business" style:
    - Tamiko Kelley
    - Laura Occhipinti
    - Many options in the birth world including our Elite NCS™/Master NCS® program

NOTES:

_____

_____

_____

_____

Managing Multiples

MARLY DRISKELL

Managing Multiples

Notice these major ideas in this segment:

- Listening to the Parents & Being a Team
- Contract
- Scrubs
- Helpful hints
- Feeding
- Changing
- Crying
- Reflux / Sleep Apnea

Nanny Marly

- ▷ INA NOTY 2015
- ▷ Certified Professional Nanny (National Academy of Nannies, Inc.)

NOTES:

_____

_____

_____

_____

Listening to the Parents & Being a Team

We all have our own ways of doing things.

- Sharing with parents to determine the methods that work best
    - Some involved in every aspect of care
    - Some will tell you about the babies' day and then go to bed
- Send a list of your "must haves"

NOTES:

48

Listening to the Parents & Being a Team

We all have our own ways of doing things.

- Keep a detailed log of events
    - I often take notes on my phone and e-mail them to the parents the next morning
- Extinction
    - I wasn't comfortable with full extinction plan
    - I worked with the parents to develop a "weaning" plan that started several weeks prior to the extinction weekend

NOTES:

_____

_____

_____

_____

_____

Contract

Everyone should execute a contract that is specific to their needs

▷ Retainer Fee

   ▷ The retainer fee is based on a week of the agreed upon salary. The fee is returned at the next to last week of employment in lieu of pay.

      ▷ Guarantee family is serious about hiring the NCS

      ▷ Guarantee NCS will be available

      ▷ Guarantee that a two-week notice of end of employment will be given by the family. Allows for preparation of new employment

NOTES:

Scrubs

- Made to repel blood
- Great advertising
- Super comfortable
- Relatively inexpensive
- Select dark colors especially for overnight work. Makes it harder for baby to see me
- Looks professional – every client has commented about how professional I look in my scrubs
- Long lasting

NOTES:

_____

_____

_____

_____

Helpful Hints

Alphabetical Order

Always place the babies in alphabetical order. Everyone interacting with the babies will be able to identify each baby. Birth order is not recommended because usually only the parents and maybe the grandparents will remember in which order they were born. You will be working in a dark room, so always having the babies in a specific order is essential.

Having the babies in order helps to remember:

- Feeding with different formulas
- Changing
- Cribs
- Medications

NOTES:

_____

_____

_____

_____

_____

Helpful Hints (con't)

Color Coded

Having each baby assigned a specific color is very helpful. This allows everyone to know which baby should be getting specific bottles, lovies, pacifiers, and clothes.

Rooms

▷ Place the cribs in a small room that is only used for sleeping

▷ Convert the dining room into a "baby" room by removing all furniture. Add

   ▷ Dresser

   ▷ Changing stations

   ▷ Gliders/rocking chairs

   ▷ Blankets

▷ 2nd bedroom for babies that are sleeping through the night. This will keep them from being awakened by the crying babies.

NEWBORN
CARE SOLUTIONS

NOTES:

53

Feeding

Once you have more babies than arms, things get a bit tricky. Depending on the parent's and pediatrician's wishes, prop feeding is very common.

Daytime interactions with volunteers

Volunteers want to help by:

▷ Often doing laundry

▷ Feeding babies

▷ Snuggle time is one-on-one

▷ Washing and preparing bottles

NOTES:

_____

_____

_____

_____

_____

Feeding (con't)

Encourage parent to pump at night according to their body's needs while allowing me to set the babies' feeding schedules

Be prepared – If the babies are eating at 10 PM, start prepping at 9:45.

Volunteers want to help by:

Options for warming bottles

▷ Baby Brezza is like a Kuerig for babies. They may go through a can of formula a day.

▷ At least 2 bottle warmers

▷ Perhaps using a crock pot for all of the bottles at one time.

NOTES:

_____

_____

_____

_____

Feeding (con't)

I lay out Boppies on the floor and sit in the middle of them. I place burp clothes and bibs on each of them.

- Why use Boppies:
  - Keeps the babies elevated, snug, and can flip them onto their bellies with gentle pressure so they can burp while others are being fed.
- Often these babies will have reflux issues, using the Boppies will allow them to be upright for the recommended 20 to 30 minutes.

NOTES:

Changing

It is basically an assembly line. Do the same for each baby.

▷ Get 1st baby

  ▷ Change diaper – don't change again after feeding unless one has pooped (Quad's dad)

  ▷ Reswaddle

  ▷ Place bib

  ▷ Place on Boppy

NOTES:

Changing (con't)

- I use muslin blankets to prop the babies because they are easy to move into position and provide a great angle so the baby doesn't get air while sucking.

- Swaddling: Everyone has their favorite method. With multiples, I use the Miracle Blanket and wrap them like little baby burritos. The Miracle Blanket doesn't have a Velcro closure so there isn't a loud sound that may wake the other babies.

NOTES:

_____

_____

_____

_____

_____

Crying

▷ You want to catch the one crying before the others awake. For one set of my quints, I had 20 seconds to get a pacifier in place or all of the others would wake up.

▷ If they are all crying, I try to "fix" the one that is most easily soothed. Then I can focus on the one that needs most of my attention.

▷ You can move two into one crib so that you can soothe both at one time.

NOTES:

Reflux / Sleep Apnea

Often high level multiples are preemies that have acid reflux and sleep apnea. All of "mine" have had reflux issues. They are usually on Prevacid or Zantac.

The babies who suffer from acid reflux need to be propped upright for 20 to 30 minutes after feedings. Placing the baby in a Boppy is most helpful.

NOTES:

_____

_____

_____

_____

_____

Reflux / Sleep Apnea (con't)

Many of the preemies will have sleep apnea and must use machines to alert when babies are not breathing correctly.

- White wire is placed under the right arm
- The bank is placed across chest
- Slip your 2nd finger between the band and the baby's chest for correct tightness. The clearance should not be too tight or too loose. If it is too loose, the machine will sound false alarms
- Often false alarms – once with a triplet, it wasn't a false alarm.

NOTES:

Working in a
HP/HNW Home

Working in a HP/HNW Home

Notice these major ideas in this segment:

▷ Interview Info / Questions

▷ Negotiations

▷ Once Hired

Interview Info / Questions

- Agency info/Research the principals
- Live in or out position, overnight accommodations, private areas how to access and when
- Family dynamics (how many, ages, live in, how often visited)
- Pets (how many, type, disposition, your role in care)
- Size of home
- Staff – who, when, where and how long?
- Other homes (size, staff, when and how often used)

NOTES:

_____

_____

_____

_____

_____

Interview Info / Questions (con't)

- Vehicle use, your own, paid mileage or company car to use
- Formal or informal household
- Guest visits, events
- Cooking (how often, food allergies, organic, vegan, likes/dislikes)
- Chain of command, report to who-principal, staff
- Your responsibilities outside of newborn care

NOTES:

_____

_____

_____

_____

_____

Negotiations

- Hours/overnights/meals
- Salary/overnight/overtime
- Medical/dental
- 401k
- Mileage
- Cell phone
- Bonus
- Travel/meals
- Growth/future

NOTES:

Once Hired

- NDA/social media, travel
- Communication with principals/staff, meetings, email, text
- Security team, access and alarm codes, emergency procedures, panic room, first aid/CPR, AED (automated external defibrillators, nearest hospital)
- Floor plan of house, access when and where

NOTES:

Once Hired (con't)

- ▷ Staff, learn from existing, team player, all to do with your kids take care of, if free time help others, work with staff not just for principals
- ▷ Travel, car seats, private jet (1st aboard), hotel or home, baby needs/emergencies...
- ▷ Projects, vendors...kids areas, timing, location, chemicals
- ▷ Relatives, who, where and when? Assist them to the degree that makes them happy

NOTES:

Infant Feeding

TONYA SAKOWICZ
NEWBORN CARE SOLUTIONS

Infant Feeding

Notice these major ideas in this segment:

▶ Human Milk Composition

▶ Is human milk beneficial (vs. formulas)

▶ What is present in human milk that cannot be replicated in formulas?

▶ History of Formula

▶ Different types of formula

Infant Feeding

- ▷ Nursing, Commercial Formulas and Alternatives
- ▷ Newborn Care Solutions Foundational Training Class
- ▷ Advanced NCS Training Class
- ▷ Elite Y2
- ▷ Other Programs

NOTES:

Human Milk Composition

- Water, fat, carbohydrates, protein, vitamins and minerals, amino acids, enzymes, and white blood cells.

- Fats: Primary source of calories, help with absorption of fat soluble vitamins, and essential for proper brain, retina and nervous system development. While specifically cutting fat does not affect a parent's milk production, calorie cutting can.

- Carbohydrates: Lactose (milk sugar) compromises about 40% of the calories. Lactose decreases unhealthy bacteria and promotes absorption of calcium, phosphorus and magnesium.

NOTES:

Human Milk Composition (con't)

- Protein: Two types—whey (60-80%) and casein (20-40%). This balance allows for quick and easy digestion. Formula often has a difference balance, inhibiting absorption.
- Proteins have great infection protection properties
- Lactoferrin inhibits the growth of iron-dependent bad bacteria such as yeast and coliforms
- Secretory IgA helps to protect the newborn against infectious viruses and bacteria, including E coli. and allergies

NEWBORN
CARE SOLUTIONS

NOTES:

_____

_____

_____

_____

NEWBORN
CARE SOLUTIONS

Human Milk Composition (con't)

- Immunoglobulins IgG and IgM protect against viral and bacterial infections.
- Eating fish increases these proteins in human milk.
- Lysozyme is an enzyme that protects against E Coli and Salmonella, promotes the growth of healthy intestinal flora and has anti-inflammatory properties.
- Bifidus Factor supports the growth of lactobactillus, creating an acidic environment where harmful bacteria cannot survive.

NOTES:

Human Milk Composition (con't)

▷ Vitamins and minerals are directly related to parent's intake

▷ Often Lactation Consultants and Doctors have parents continue prenatal vitamins to ensure adequate vitamins for both parent and baby

▷ Fat Soluble Vitamins present are A, D, E and K and are vital to infant health

▷ Water Soluble are Vitamin C, Riboflavin, Niacin and Panthothenic Acid

NOTES:

_____

_____

_____

_____

_____

What else may be present in human milk?

- Food proteins, particularly dairy, soy, and peanuts, pass through human milk
- Vitamins, including iron supplements
- Medications (some are safe while nursing, many are not)
- Herbs (some are helpful with lactation, many are harmful to an infant or can interact)

NOTES:

What else may be present in human milk? (con't)

- ▶ Caffeine (keep it at under 300 mg—three 5 ounce cups) per day)
- ▶ Nicotine (linked to colic like symptoms, reflux and respiratory illness)
- ▶ THC (the active component in marijuana) at 8 times the level present in bloodstream

NOTES:

_____

_____

_____

_____

_____

Is human milk beneficial (vs. formulas)

- In a word—Yes!
- Protects against infection
- Contains Antibodies
- Reduces later health issues such as diabetes, obesity and asthma
- Proteins are more easily digested
- Calcium and Iron in human milk are more easily absorbed

NOTES:

_____

_____

_____

_____

_____

What is present in human milk that cannot be replicated in formulas?

- Over 100 ingredients that cannot be replicated in formula
- Even though the main components are similar, there are significant differences in the types of carbohydrates, proteins, vitamins and minerals
- Levels and quality are superior in human milk and contributes to a larger (smarter) brain in nursed babies, even in the short term
- Formula has higher levels, but it is less absorbable, so human milk yields higher protein and iron to babies

NOTES:

_____

_____

_____

_____

_____

What are other benefits of human milk?

▷ Live antibodies passed from parent to baby

▷ Proper levels of vitamins and minerals

▷ Parent/baby bonding

▷ Lower infant mortality rates (in developing countries—6-25 times more likely to die on formula)

NOTES:

_____

_____

_____

_____

_____

What are other benefits of human milk? (con't)

- Physical benefits to the parent:
    - Prolactin and oxytocin release into the parent's body
    - Quicker recovery from birth
    - Lower rates of breast and ovarian cancer
    - Lower rates of Type 2 diabetes, rheumatoid arthritis, cardiovascular disease, high blood pressure and high cholesterol

NOTES:

_____

_____

_____

_____

_____

History of Formula

- Throughout history, we see records of parents who could not nurse utilizing wet nurses

- "Dry Nursing" or preparing a homemade baby 'food' was less common- ingredients were based on region and economic status of the family

- In the early 19th century in both America and Europe, wet nurses began to fall out of favor and more homemade options were used

- The first "India Rubber Nipple" was invented in 1845 and the use of homemade options really began to rise.

NOTES:

History of Formula (con't)

- Within a year, physicians began to note a sharp rise in infant illness and mortality

- In 1867, Justin von Liebig invented the first commercial infant formula, Liebig's Soluble Food for Babies

- Others quickly followed: Mellins Infant Food, Ridges Food for Infants and one that is still around today: Nestle'

NOTES:

_____

_____

_____

_____

History of Formula (con't)

▷ In 1890, Thomas Morgan Rotch published a home recipe called a percentage formula that listed specific percentages of cow's milk, water, cream and sugar or honey to more closely approximate what they thought was in human milk and babies could digest

▷ While most babies were still nursed, percentage formulas increased in popularity, along with more illness: Scurvy, rickets and bacterial infections

▷ Around 1920, they discovered adding orange juice and cod-liver oil greatly decreased these problem

NOTES:

History of Formula (con't)

- In the late 1920's through the 1950's, evaporated milk became widely available and it was the most frequent choice for homemade formula, especially when initial studies appeared to show babies did just as well on this as human milk (now proven not to be true)

- Similac (similar to lactation) and Sobee first came onto the market in the 1920's, but evaporated milk formula dominated until the 1950's

- In 1951 Similac was reformulated to closer mimic human milk and in 1959, Enfamil (infant meal) came onto the market

NOTES:

_____

_____

_____

_____

_____

History of Formula (con't)

- Through the 1950's and 60's, heavy marketing through doctor's offices helped to increase the use of commercial formulas and by the late 60's the use of homemade options dropped off immensely

- Generic Brand formulas did not appear until the late 1990's

- While we have seen a resurgence in breastfeeding, formula feeding still dominates the market world-wide, particularly in developed countries

- Globally, infant formula (0-6 months) is an 8 billion dollar market

NOTES:

Dairy Based Formulas

- Roughly designed to be based on "human milk" at approximately 3 months post-partum
- Whey and Casein are the protein source, a blend of vegetable oils as the fat source, lactose as the carbohydrate source, and a vitamin/mineral blend, plus other ingredients depending on the manufacturer.
- Corn Syrup is often the first listed ingredient in formulas
- Soy is a close follower, even in dairy based formulas

NOTES:

_____

_____

_____

_____

_____

Dairy Based Formulas (con't)

▷ Babies tend to sleep longer because the proteins are much harder to digest—Little Miss Muffet

▷ Dairy formula fed babies tend to have larger heads because of the steroids in cows milk

▷ Babies often eat less as it takes less to fill them up and they digest it slower

▷ Bowel movements tend to be more solid and adult like than nursed or even organic formula fed babies

NOTES:

_____

_____

_____

_____

_____

Dairy Based Formulas (con't)

▷ Many babies do not handle dairy-based proteins well and show signs similar to reflux

▷ Dairy is the most common protein allergy in infants

▷ If an infant has a milk protein intolerance, it can damage the gut, ranging from diarrhea to blood in the stool

▷ Milk protein intolerance is very common in infants and children under age 3

NOTES:

_____

_____

_____

_____

_____

Soy based formula

- ▷ Soy formula uses processed ground soybeans as the main source of protein
- ▷ Still nearly 50% corn syrup and sugar
- ▷ Highly controversial because of Isoflavones, a compound found in legumes
- ▷ Genestein, the main Isoflavone in soy byproducts, is also called a phytoestrogen because it mimics estrogen in the body at the level of 5 birth control pills per day

NOTES:

_____

_____

_____

_____

Soy based formula (con't)

- ▶ Babies fed exclusively soy formula have 13,000-22,000 times higher levels of Isoflavones in their bloodstream than breastfed or dairy-based formula fed babies.

- ▶ Infants in particular are especially sensitive to the introduction of soy at certain developmental points and the effects of this excess estrogen exposure may not be detectable for many years

NEWBORN
CARE SOLUTIONS

NOTES:

_____

_____

_____

_____

_____

NEWBORN
CARE SOLUTIONS

Possible Side Effects of Soy

▷ Early onset of puberty in girls; delayed or absence of puberty in boys

▷ Alteration in the development of breast tissue

▷ Inhibition of brain growth because of Trypsin Inhibitors

▷ Phytic acid in soy inhibits the absorption of iron, calcium, magnesium and zinc, even to the point of zinc deficiency and lowered IQ

▷ Unexplained Infertility

▷ Cancer of the Reproductive organs

NOTES:

_____

_____

_____

_____

Hypoallergenic Formulas

▷ Hypoallergenic formulas have "hydrolyzed" or "pre-digested" proteins, or broken down proteins to make them tiny and less likely to prompt an allergic reaction

▷ This requires intense processing, resulting in a bitter, unpleasant taste

▷ Because the lactose is removed in this process, manufacturers substitute with sugar, corn syrup and tapioca

▷ These formulas are 30-90% higher in salt

NOTES:

Hypoallergenic Formulas (con't)

- Pregestamil, one type of hypoallergenic formula has Medium Chain Triglycerides, a type of fat easier to digest for babies with fat malabsorption disorders—while it can help with weight gain, it is not a 'naturally occurring" fat and effects are unknown

- MCT's are also hard on the liver—these formulas should never be given unless doctor prescribed because of the possible effects on the intestinal system and liver if they are not needed

- MCT's have no essential fatty acids, critical to a growing babies brain

- Hypoallergenic formulas are very expensive, sometimes up to 4-5 times more expensive than standard formula

NOTES:

Other Commercial Options

▷ Food allergies, malabsorption issues, other medical conditions all can require specialty formulas and companies make one for just about everything, even adding many things that have absolutely no backing in science for what they are used for (DHA/ARA example)

▷ Manufacturers are creating new products all the time. You can now find specialty formulas just for newborns, just for supplementing, for toddlers, for reflux, for constipation, organic and even non organic non GMO formulas

NOTES:

_____

_____

_____

_____

_____

Organic Formulas

- Organic formulas have the same plusses and minuses that any other commercially made formula does—the main difference is the source of the ingredients
- To be labeled organic (not "natural—don't be fooled), a product must be:
- Non GMO
- Not raised or grown with added hormones or antibiotics
- Not sprayed with non-approved pesticides
- Given organic feed or started from an organic seed

NOTES:

Organic Formulas (con't)

- So is organic worth all the hype?
- Organic foods have been shown to have higher nutritional values and higher levels of antioxidants than non organic through over 200 studies in the BJN
- Dairy in particular is important as so many of the hormones given to cows pass through their milk and into our food supply
- Antibiotics in dairy also pass through and are considered

NEWBORN
CARE SOLUTIONS

NOTES:

_____

_____

_____

_____

_____

NEWBORN
CARE SOLUTIONS

Homemade Formulas

- Homemade formulas were once the norm and they are coming back
- There are multiple sources online for various recipes using cows milk, goats milk and even paleo recipes using no milk at all
- There are concerns about making homemade formula, but those concerns usually rise from lack of knowledge
- Some doctors will not approve of this—be careful
- Do not make homemade formula as an NCS—ask the parent to prepare it— you simply feed it

NOTES:

Homemade Dairy Formula

- Most recipes use RAW (unpasteurized) milk—ideally organic--from grass fed cows
- Raw milk has not had all the helpful enzymes and bacteria destroyed through the pasteurization process and so is much easier to digest
- Even many babies who have been diagnosed with dairy allergies can tolerate raw milk very well

NOTES:

Homemade Goats Milk Formula

▷ Dr. Sears recommends goats milk over cows milk based homemade formulas because of the higher nutritional content and closer similarity to human milk

▷ Goats milk is lower in folic acid though, so it must be added to the formula

▷ Raw, unpasteurized goats milk is your best option, but hard to find and spoils easily

NOTES:

_____

_____

_____

_____

_____

Homemade Goats Milk Formula (con't)

- ▷ Powdered goats milk is the next best option
- ▷ Dr. Sears recipes: http://www.askdrsears.com/topics/feeding-eating/feeding-infants-toddlers/goat-milk
- ▷ My favorite recipe: http://www.passionatehomemaking.com/2009/11/goats-milk-formula-natural-supplementation-for-baby.html

NOTES:

_____

_____

_____

_____

Homemade Paleo Formula

- Uses beef or chicken livers simmered in homemade, low sodium beef or chicken stock

- It is pureed and then has multiple vitamins and minerals and live cultures and probiotics added

- Healthy fats are added through coconut oil, olive oil, expeller pressed sunflower oil and cod liver oil

- http://www.westonaprice.org/beginner-videos/baby-formula-video-by-sarah-pope-2/

- Controversial as many doctors do not agree with a paleo lifestyle and therefore automatically dismiss this as a possible option

NEWBORN
CARE SOLUTIONS

NOTES:

_____

_____

_____

_____

_____

NEWBORN
CARE SOLUTIONS

How do we support a nursing client?

- ▷ Be sure to educate yourself on as much as possible regarding nursing
- ▷ Limit your advice to that which you are properly trained and certified for—refer anything else to a lactation professional
- ▷ Support and encourage the parent's efforts in a gentle, but non-pushy manner
- ▷ Bring baby to the parent at night, ready to feed, then step aside but stay within the parent's field of vision or close ear shot so if the parent has struggles or needs you, you are available

NOTES:

How do we support a nursing client? (con't)

- Be sure to encourage her to eat well, drink lots of fluids and get adequate rest
- Be sure that if she opts to stop nursing for any reason, you are careful to never come across as negative or judgmental regarding her decision, no matter how you feel

NOTES:

How do we support a nursing client? (con't)

- ▸ If the parent is opting to nurse multiples, discuss with the parent in advance how the parent plans to do this
- ▸ If the parent opts to nurse 2 at once, strongly encourage the parent to seek the advice of an experienced lactation professional who can teach the parent various holds
- ▸ If the parent opts to nurse 1 per feeding, encourage the parent to pump if they want human milk fed to the other baby in a bottle or to select the healthiest formula option she feels safe with for the other bab(ies).
- ▸ Remind her that even the smallest amount of human milk has positive benefits for her children

NOTES:

_____

_____

_____

_____

_____

So What IS the best option?

- As with all things babies, the best option is what allows for a healthy, growing, well-rested baby and well-rested family
- Each family has to make their own final decision with the help of their healthcare provider
- We can educate, but we cannot diagnose or prescribe
- We must support the parents decision and if we feel we can't, then we need to politely and respectfully move on

NOTES:

Working with Preemies

ANNIE DUGUID

Working with Preemies

Notice these major ideas in this segment:

- General Care
- Feeding / Nursing
- Trauma and Psych Issues
- Medical

General Care

- Head shape and frequent and equal moving
- Back sleeping problems- not enough tummy time
- Physical and developmental problems
- Low lights-peds office Low noise and white noise
- Skin care
- Cleaning in preemie folds

NOTES:

_____

_____

_____

_____

_____

General Care (con't)

- ▷ Concerns with apnea monitor probes
- ▷ Bathing and warmth of water, room, change table, hats and check temp afterwards
- ▷ Skin care with billi lights - no tanning oil :)
- ▷ Nontoxic environment - why its more important for preemies
- ▷ Grounding post NICU to get rid of EMF overload
- ▷ Increased positional breathing risks with preemies

NOTES:

Feeding / Nursing

- Going up in feeds slowly 60, 75, 90, 105, 120, 150, 170 or 180
- Preemie formulas
- Fortifying milk and higher fat human milk
- You can restart breastfeeding even after a long time
- Importance of mother pumping

NOTES:

_____

_____

_____

_____

_____

Feeding / Nursing (con't)

- Importance of skin on skin on parent's human milk supply
- Haberman feeders
- Syringe Feeding
  (video: https://www.youtube.com/watch?v=90l78o-bfPo)
- Other nipples: Hospital "preemie" – easy flow, Dr Browns, "preemie" slow flow

NOTES:

_____

_____

_____

_____

Trauma and Psych Issues

Babies increased risk of attachment issues (Reactive Attachment Disorder) with NICU or medical issues, esp. those involving unresolved pain.

- Pacifiers
- Sugar
- Warmth
- Swaddling
- kin-to-skin

NOTES:

_____

_____

_____

_____

_____

Trauma and Psych Issues (con't)

- ▷ Exposure to trauma triggers flight or fright mode
- ▷ Babies can get stuck
- ▷ 9/11 babies had high cortisol from mothers trauma
- ▷ Generational trauma

NOTES:

_____

_____

_____

_____

Trauma and Psych Issues (con't)

- Balancing good sleep habits with undoing trauma
- Increased need to 'attachment parent' preemies, surrogate, and adopted babies (long term RAD is worse than sleeping issues) while still doing what you can to encourage good sleep
- Brain 'pruning' and importance of ensure that the right things will be hardwired while bad stuff is 'pruned'

NOTES:

_____

_____

_____

_____

_____

Trauma and Psych Issues (con't)

Parents who've experienced loss or fear from NICU and have increased chance of PTSD and mood disorders

▸ Nervous and withdrawn mothers

▸ Need more encouragement

▸ Skin on skin

▸ Increased risk of PPD or attachment issues

▸ Risk is higher if mother had serious health issues

NOTES:

_____

_____

_____

_____

_____

Medical

Resuscitation

- Importance of neonatal specific training
- Frequently review and practice
- Emergency contacts – have handy for medical emergencies
- Numbers for NICU nurses and doctors in case of questions
- Oral motor issues – causes and feeding solutions and therapies
- Probiotics - were they given in NICU? Request ped to consider if not – in NZ and other areas, they are given routinely

NOTES:

Medical (con't)

Resuscitation (con't)

▷ Knowledge of common drugs given in NICU and the potential side effects

▷ Knowledge of common drugs babies can come home on and potential side effects

▷ Knowledge of medical procedures done in NICU and potential side effects

▷ Increased risk of RSV and other illnesses

▷ What to do with parents or friends and relatives who ignore the risks

NOTES:

Medical (con't)

Signs of feeding issues:

▷ NEC

▷ Pyloric Stenosis

▷ Reflux

▷ Biliary atresia (not sure if this is something always picked up by hospitals or common enough to mention, but its fatal if not treated early)

NOTES:

_____

_____

_____

_____

_____

Medical (con't)

Signs of feeding issues (con't):

▷ Heart problems

▷ Coming home on apnea monitors

▷ Coming home on oxygen – too high can make a preemie 'forget' to breath

▷ Jaundice- signs and symptoms – check in natural daylight

NOTES:

_____

_____

_____

_____

_____

Car Seat Safety

LISA COTE
CPST & SPECIAL NEEDS CERTIFIED

NEWBORN
CARE SOLUTIONS

Car Seat Safety

Notice these major ideas in this segment:

- How to select a car seat
- Car seat angle tolerance test
- How to restrain baby in car seat
- Basics of car seat installation
- Other safety considerations of car seat use

Lisa Cote

- Child Passenger Safety Technician
- Special Needs Trained

NOTES:

_____

_____

_____

_____

_____

We Will Discuss:

- How to select a car seat
- Car seat angle tolerance test
- How to restrain baby in car seat
- Basics of car seat installation
- Other safety considerations of car seat use

NOTES:

_____

_____

_____

_____

Car Seat Selection

- Select a car seat that the child meets the weight and height requirements of.
- Many infant only seats (or Rear Facing Only) start at 4lbs and fit preemies well.
- A seat that fits the vehicle the child will be riding in.
- Parents will likely need to test fit seats in their vehicle to assure a proper fit.

IS YOUR CHILD IN THE RIGHT CAR SEAT?

SAFERCAR.GOV/THERIGHTSEAT

NEWBORN
CARE SOLUTIONS

NOTES:

NEWBORN
CARE SOLUTIONS

Car Seat Selection (con't)

- ▷ A seat that fits the parents budget.
- ▷ There are a wide variety of seats available in a wide variety of price ranges.
- ▷ A seat the parents will use correctly 100% of the time.
- ▷ http://carseatblog.com/safest-recommended-car-seats/

NOTES:

_____

_____

_____

_____

_____

The Angle Tolerance Test

- Performed on NICU babies that have concerns of breathing issues and/or will remain on oxygen.
- Some hospitals will perform this test on every baby leaving the NICU no matter what.
- The ATT must be performed with the seat the child will be riding in, must be performed on a hard flat surface, and at the appropriate 45° angle.

NOTES:

The Angle Tolerance Test (con't)

- The ATT should be performed for no less than 90 minutes.
- If baby fails the ATT, it is preferred that baby remain in the NICU a while longer.
- Use of a car bed should be a last resort for baby.

Image from PreventtInjury.comry.com

NEWBORN
CARE SOLUTIONS

NOTES:

_____

_____

_____

_____

_____

NEWBORN
CARE SOLUTIONS

Proper Fitting of Baby to Seat

- ▷ Baby must be seated with bottom scooted all the way into back of the seat.
- ▷ Harness straps must come from at or below baby's shoulders while Rear Facing (RF).
  - ▷ This helps in preventing baby from ramping up the seat in a crash and protecting the head.

NOTES:

_____

_____

_____

_____

Proper Fitting of Baby to Seat (con't)

- Harness must always be tightened snugly with no pinchable slack at the shoulders and the retainer clip (chest clip) placed at armpit level.
- If child needs extra support in their seat, rolled receiving blankets are allowed to be placed on either side of the baby.
  - No aftermarket head supports or inserts are allowed to be used.

NOTES:

126

Basics of Car Seat Installation

▷ Always read the manual to BOTH the car seat and the vehicle.
▷ Center installation is the preferred location but proper installation, whether it be center or outboard, overrides that.

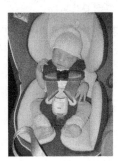

NOTES:

_____

_____

_____

_____

_____

Basics of Car Seat Installation

▷ With multiple car seats it is important that each seat is independently installed correctly.

    ▷ Meaning one seat cannot be helping another be secure. The car seats are not allowed to overlap each other nor press tightly against each other.

▷ Use of seat belt OR Lower Anchors are equally safe. The one that offers better/correct install would be the ideal one to choose.

    ▷ Never use seat belt or lower anchors together.

NEWBORN
CARE SOLUTIONS

NOTES:

_____

_____

_____

_____

NEWBORN
CARE SOLUTIONS

Other Car Seat Safety Considerations

- Utilize the car seat as little as possible.
  - Emphasize that car seats are for travel, not for play, sleeping, or feeding.
- Car seats are not made to be utilized on the tops of shopping carts.
  - Doing this can damage the locking mechanism of the seat onto its base.
- Baby should always be properly buckled in the seat any time it's in use.
- During cold months, baby should not wear thick winter outerwear as this can create a false impression of a properly tightened harness.

Happy Car Seating

NOTES:

Problems in the NCS World

TONYA SAKOWICZ
NEWBORN CARE SOLUTIONS

Problems in the NCS World

Notice these major ideas in this segment:

- Legal
- Client
- Placement and Referral Agencies
- Other NCS

Legal

- ▷ Use of the words Baby Nurse and Babynurse
- ▷ Referral Fees
- ▷ Contracts vs. Work Agreements
- ▷ Retainers/Deposits/Booking Fees
- ▷ Cancellations
- ▷ Lawsuits

Where do I get help?

NOTES:

_____

_____

_____

_____

Client

- ▷ Reluctant/Refuse to sign work agreement
- ▷ Changing items on the agreement before signing
- ▷ Changing things up after you start
- ▷ Postpartum Mood Disorders
- ▷ Unsafe practices in the home

Where do I get help?

NOTES:

_____

_____

_____

_____

_____

Placement and Referral Agencies

▷ Doesn't truly understand the role of an NCS

▷ Having you fill out a nanny application

▷ Refusing to understand you cannot give out HP client info

▷ Giving client wrong information

▷ Refusing to allow deposit collection/NCS work agreement

Where do I get help?

NOTES:

_____

_____

_____

_____

Other NCS

- Gossip, Bad-Mouthing and Rumors
- Stealing your information/web content/work agreement
- Infringing on Trademarks
- Unprofessional conduct on and off the job
- Violating an NDA
- Territorial

Where do I get help?

NOTES:

_____

_____

_____

_____

_____

Alternative Care
Options

TONYA SAKOWICZ
NEWBORN CARE SOLUTIONS

NEWBORN
CARE SOLUTIONS

Alternative Care Options

Notice these major ideas in this segment:

▷ Nursed baby is not gaining well or has lost weight in the few days following birth

▷ Baby has reflux

▷ Baby is congested

▷ What other things can chiropractic help with for baby?

▷ What other things can cranial-sacral therapy help with?

▷ What other things can human milk help with?

Alternative Care Options

Problem: Nursed baby is not gaining well or has lost weight in the few days following birth

Traditional Response: Supplement with formula

Alternative Response Options:

▷ Was mom on IV fluids in the hospital during labor? Baby can have "artificial" gain and loss: wait

▷ Is baby nursing effectively, long enough with a proper latch? This needs to be referred to a breastfeeding specialist, ideally an IBCLC

▷ Does that baby have tongue or lip tie? This needs to be evaluated by someone highly experienced; find a good doc in the area

NOTES:

Alternative Care Options

Problem: Nursed baby is not gaining well or has lost weight in the few days following birth

Traditional Response: Supplement with formula

Alternative Response Options:

▷ Have the baby evaluated by another doctor in the practice who is more pro-nursing

▷ Find a way to use donor breastmilk and encourage mom to syringe feed if appropriate

▷ If formula is the only option, try to encourage them to use organic or non-US formulas

NEWBORN
CARE SOLUTIONS

NOTES:

_____

_____

_____

_____

NEWBORN
CARE SOLUTIONS

Alternative Care Options (con't)

Problem: Baby has reflux

Traditional Response: Zantac (acid reducer) or Prevacid (Proton Pump Inhibitor)

Alternative Response Options:

▷ Remove the two most common "protein" intolerance issues from mom's diet

▷ If formula feeding, switch to an organic, non-US or hypoallergenic

▷ Consider crano-sacral therapy

▷ Consider chiropractic

▷ Amber bead necklaces

▷ Vinegar

▷ Compounded medications

▷ Other home remedies

▷ Evaluate and Correct for Oral Ties

NOTES:

Alternative Care Options (con't)

Problem: Baby is congested

Traditional Response: Saline rinse

Alternative Response Options:

- Essential Oils, particularly Eucalyptus and Lemon
- Determine the cause—possibly mom's diet
- If virus is suspected, mixing breastmilk into the saline rinse
- Steamy bathroom
- If bottle fed, serving colder than normal

NOTES:

Alternative Care Options (con't)

What other things can chiropractic help with for baby?

- Ear Infections
- General fussiness
- Birth trauma

NOTES:

_____

_____

_____

_____

_____

Alternative Care Options (con't)

What other things can cranial-sacral therapy help with?

- Birth trauma from extraction or c-section delivery
- Constipation
- Reflux
- Gas
- Sleep
- Teething pain
- Head shape issues
- Ear aches
- Developmental delays

NOTES:

_____

_____

_____

_____

_____

Alternative Care Options (con't)

What other things can essential oils help with?

- Sleep
- Relaxation
- Infections and more

NOTES:

_____

_____

_____

_____

_____

Alternative Care Options (con't)

What other things can human milk help with?

- Pink eye
- Preventing and healing diaper rash
- Acne
- Eczema and cradle cap
- Pain relief
- Ear infections
- Cuts
- Scrapes
- Itching of pox
- Insect bites and more

NOTES:

Advanced Sleep Conditioning for Newborn Care Specialists

TONYA SAKOWICZ
NEWBORN CARE SOLUTIONS

Advanced Sleep Conditioning for Newborn Care Specialists

Notice these major ideas in this segment:

- Sleep Goals and Family Needs
- What's Always the Same?
- Sleep Facts
- Causes of Night Waking
- Steps to Successful Infant Sleep

Sleep Goals and Family Needs

- ▶ Each family will have different sleep goals depending on their beliefs and circumstances
- ▶ Parents of multiples or families where both parents must return to work fairly quickly usually are more motivated to have baby STTN sooner
- ▶ Mothers with babies who sleep well have lower rates of Post Partum Depression
- ▶ Well rested babies lead to more well rested families
- ▶ Well rested babies grow better

NOTES:

_____

_____

_____

_____

_____

What's Always the Same?

Regardless of sleep goals, some things should always be consistent:

- Good solid daytime feedings to meet 24 hour calorie needs during the daytime hours

- Little to no snacking, especially if breastfeeding

- Encourage cluster feeding when it occurs—it helps with supply

- Follow a consistent pattern of Eat, Play, Sleep, even if not actively sleep conditioning as it sets the pattern for both parents and baby

- Follow the same simple routine before every sleep period so baby begins to learn these steps indicate "sleep"

NOTES:

Sleep Facts

Regardless of sleep goals, some things should always be consistent:

▷ Infant sleep is different than adult sleep

▷ Circadian Rhythm is different including Melatonin production and cortisol production

▷ Sleep Cycle length is different

▷ Infants enter sleep differently

▷ Initially babies usually come fully wake between sleep cycles

▷ Babies often need help learning to stay asleep between sleep cycles

NOTES:

_____

_____

_____

_____

_____

Sleep Facts (con't)

 ▷ Babies have twice as much lighter sleep than adults

 ▷ This lighter sleep has a purpose—survival

 ▷ It also aids brain development as neuro pathways and nerve proteins (the brains building blocks) are developed during this time—the brain doesn't rest during active REM sleep and so it develops during this time of rapid growth

 ▷ Preemies spend even more time in the REM sleep mode—up to 90% of their sleep can be REM sleep because the primary need of a preemie is growth

NOTES:

Sleep Facts (con't)

▷ Active (REM) sleep = brain growth / quiet or NREM sleep = brain restoration

▷ Though it varies based on a variety of factors, most babies can be naturally encouraged to sleep through the night without "crying it out" somewhere around 12 weeks of age (assuming term—adjust for preemies), so long as they are approximately 12 lbs and have no major health issues

▷ At this same age, babies sleep entry also changes and they progress to deep sleep much more quickly

▷ Even a baby with good sleep conditioning will still wake at night on occasion

NOTES:

_____

_____

_____

_____

Causes of Night Waking

- Pain—teething, reflux, growth and injury can cause pain and pain will wake a sleeping baby more often
- Illness and fever
- Hunger—if the baby is not having their calorie needs met during the day, they will wake at night to meet that need
- Neurological issues we cannot yet see
- Developmental milestones, both physical and cognitive
- Unusual disturbances—babies can learn to sleep through many noises, but the sudden barking of a dog, a doorbell or other sharp, loud noise can wake them

NOTES:

Steps to Successful Infant Sleep

Recreate the womb:

▷ Dark room (use darkening shades if needed)

▷ Sound machine (80 decibels), preferably without an off timer

▷ Swaddling

▷ Proper temperature of 68-72 degrees

NOTES:

_____

_____

_____

_____

_____

Steps to Successful Infant Sleep (con't)

- Follow a pattern of eat, play, sleep
- Make sure daily caloric needs are met:
  - Weigh baby in pounds
  - Convert weight to kilograms (divide by 2.2), so 10lbs =4.55 kgs
  - Multiply weight by 120, so 4.55 x 120 = 546. This is the daily number of calories a healthy, term, 10 lb baby needs
  - If a baby is preemie or has health needs, be sure the healthcare provider is giving you the daily calorie requirements

NOTES:

_____

_____

_____

_____

_____

Steps to Successful Infant Sleep (con't)

- ▷ Have a consistent short routine prior to sleep periods
- ▷ Start your basics of lower lights, lower voices and no screen time at least 30 minutes before nighttime sleep. This helps baby know night is coming as it lowers cortisol levels
- ▷ Help baby learn to drift off to sleep on their own
- ▷ Put baby down drowsy but awake
- ▷ Try not to pick up a baby that is fussing—soothe in other ways
- ▷ At night, avoid lights, talking, singing, eye contact, etc.

NOTES:

_____

_____

_____

_____

Steps to Successful Infant Sleep (con't)

- Learn and use the 5 "S's"
- 1. Swaddle
- 2. Side or Stomach Position
- 3. Swing or Sway (jiggling works too)
- 4. Shushing
- 5. Sucking

NOTES:

_____

_____

_____

_____

_____

Steps to Successful Infant Sleep (con't)

- ▷ Using a Dream Feed
- ▷ Can help when baby doesn't meet calorie needs during the day
- ▷ Babies (and adults) naturally take one longer sleep period in a 24 hour one—it often helps baby keep that stretch between 10:30/11:00 and 6-7 am sooner

NOTES:

Steps to Successful Infant Sleep (con't)

- If baby has been consistently already been waking at say, 2 am, you may need to help hold him off for a few days, stretching his early AM feeding 15-30 mins each day until you move it later. This usually only takes a few days.

- A dream feed of expressed human milk is a great way for partners to get involved

- Dream feeds should be gradually dropped between 10-12 weeks of age

NOTES:

Steps to Successful Infant Sleep (con't)

▷ Using Wake to Sleep to lengthen night sleep and naps

  ▷ Babies who habitually wake at the same time each night and only take 30-40 minute naps can often be helped using Wake to Sleep

  ▷ A few minutes PRIOR to their habitual wake time, gently rouse the baby and then comfort them using the 5 'S's back into the next sleep cycle. You can do this night or day

  ▷ Continue using this method during their habitual wake time, gradually lessening your help as they drift back into sleep

  ▷ Usually over a period of 2-3 weeks you can break habitual waking using Wake to Sleep

NOTES:

_____

_____

_____

_____

_____

Steps to Successful Infant Sleep (con't)

- My "S's"
- Sooth; using the 5 "S's"
- Satisfy; ensure calorie needs are met
- Schedule; follow a consistent pattern with appropriate wake times during the day
- Stretch; around 6 weeks of age, begin to stretch the night time feeding by 15-30 minutes every 3-5 days depending on the babies size, growth and response to your efforts

NOTES:

_____

_____

_____

_____

_____

Steps to Successful Infant Sleep (con't)

- ▷ We've discussed soothing and satisfying, lets talk scheduling and stretching
- ▷ What should a schedule look like for a newborn:
  - ▷ Many times we need to help set the schedule as newborn sleep can be all over the map
  - ▷ The first 6 weeks are as much about the parent as they are the baby
  - ▷ Establish a fairly consistent AM wake time, even if that means waking a baby—if both parents are returning to work, try to set this time to coordinate with what time they will need to leave in the AM

NEWBORN
CARE SOLUTIONS

NOTES:

_____

_____

_____

_____

NEWBORN
CARE SOLUTIONS

Steps to Successful Infant Sleep (con't)

- ▷ Wake baby, rouse fully by unswaddling, changing diaper, washing face and feet with a cool washcloth and turning ON lights or opening curtains

- ▷ Light exposure is critical for "waking" as it stimulates cortisol production and helps your body recognize daytime, outside light is even better, especially in the afternoon

- ▷ Feed baby, working with baby as needed to get in a full feeding

NOTES:

Steps to Successful Infant Sleep (con't)

- Play and interact with baby following the feeding to stimulate and engage the brain and to help tire their bodies in preparation for nap time
- About 1 hour after waking, begin your short nap routine (should be similar to night, but it is fine to have variation)
- About 1 hour to 1 hour 15 minutes after waking, put baby down for AM nap

NOTES:

Steps to Successful Infant Sleep (con't)

- If the newborn begins to wake 30-45 mins into the nap, allow them 2 mins to attempt to resettle, but do not allow them to full-on cry
- If they cannot resettle, sooth the newborn using your 5 "S's", but try not to pick them up
- Usually they will fall back to sleep

NOTES:

_____

_____

_____

_____

_____

Steps to Successful Infant Sleep (con't)

- After 1 ½-2 hours, gently wake baby and repeat the pattern throughout the day
- At around 6 weeks, assuming baby is growing well, begin to stretch the awake time to approximately 90 mins
- At around 12-18 weeks, you can begin to stretch it to 100-120 minutes depending on the baby

NOTES:

Steps to Successful Infant Sleep (con't)

- By 4-6 months of age, most babies, assuming they are healthy, can sleep a pattern of an AM nap of 1½-2 hours, an afternoon nap of 1 ½-2 hours, a late afternoon or very early evening nap of 1 hour, and an overnight long stretch of 10-12 hours.

- Studies show that tryptophan (the amino acid that stimulates melatonin production) levels in parent's milk varies throughout the day, so if baby is fed pumped human milk, label bags by time of day and use at the same time of day whenever possible

NOTES:

Steps to Successful Infant Sleep (con't)

- ▷ Awake times at this age should be approximately 2 hours from the point of waking to the point of returning to sleep
- ▷ Every baby will vary some depending on their temperament, health, family situation and that days routine

NOTES:

_____

_____

_____

_____

Steps to Successful Infant Sleep (con't)

- Does where baby sleeps or what happens during the day matter?
- For some babies, yes, but only during the first 6 weeks or so until good patterns are established
- For some more sensitive babies, it always matters
- Occasionally you will encounter a baby who can appear to sleep anytime, anywhere—for some this is fine, for others it is not true sleep and it can disrupt night sleep significantly
- Only trial and error will tell you

NOTES:

What "If"?

- If I am doing everything right, and baby still isn't sleeping well, then what?
- Examine your log:
  - Is there anything consistently there that shows a pattern of sleep disruption (mailman, school pick-up of other kids, etc.?)
  - Is baby truly eating well during the day?
  - Is baby being put down for naps BEFORE she is overtired?
  - Is baby being picked up too quickly and not allowed to self-sooth?
  - Is baby napping somewhere other than their normal sleep location?

NOTES:

_____

_____

_____

_____

_____

What "If"? (con't)

- Is baby getting ill?
- Is baby at a possibly cognitive or developmental milestone?
- Has something changed in the home that is creating stress for the family?
  - Loss of job
  - Move
  - Vacation
  - New pet
  - Relationship Stress
  - Illness/PPD in a parent

NOTES:

Now What?

- I think I have found the problem—now what?
- Can you fix it yourself?
- Do you need to approach the parents about it?
- How do you approach the parents about it?
- What if they won't or can't fix it?
- Stay or Move on?

NOTES:

_____

_____

_____

_____

_____

Resources

Healthy Sleep Habits, Happy Child - *Dr. Marc Weissbluth*

The Happiest Baby on the Block - *Dr. Harvey Karp*

Touchpoints - *Dr. T. Berry Brazelton*

The Self-Calmed Baby - *Dr. William A.H. Sammons*

Sleeping Through the Night - *Joni A. Mindell, PhD*

Secrets of the Baby Whisperer - *Tracy Hogg and Melinda Blau*

Twelve Hours Sleep -*Twelve Weeks Old Suzy Giordano*

The Whole Person Fertility Program - *Niravi B Payne, MS*

Bright from the Start - *Jill Stamm, PhD*

Your Baby and Child - *Dr. Penelope Leach*

Colic Solved - *Dr. Brian Vartebedian*

Your Fussy Baby - *Dr. Marc Weissbluth*

Genetic Influences on EEG Sleep and the human circadian clock: a twin study Pharmacopsychiatry, 27, 7-10

Sleep Organization and Energy Expenditure of breastfed and formula fed infants Pediatric Research, 32, 514-519

The relationship between dietary components and sleep Perceptive Motor Skills, 75, 873-874

Sleep Patterns in hyperkinetic and normal children Sleep, 4, 366-384

A naturalistic assessment of the motor activity of hyperactive boys Archives of General Psychiatry, 40, 681-687

Sleep patterns, attention span, and infant temperament Journal of Developmental and Behavioral Pediatrics, 4, 34-36

Resources

Influence of gentle birth delivery procedures and other perinatal circumstances on infant temperament

Journal of Pediatrics, 108, 134-136

Infantile colic and food hypersensitivity Journal of Pediatric Gastroenterology and Nutrition, 30, S67-76

Crying in Infants and Children British Medical Journal, I, 75-75

Persistent Crying in early infancy: a non-trivial condition of risk for the developming mother-infant relationship Child: Care, Health and Development, 24, 395-424

Delayed onset of "three months" colic in premature infants American Journal of Diseases of Children, 75, 190-192

Infant sleep patterns from birth to 16 weeks of age Journal of Pediatrics, 65, 576-582

REM latency: Development in the first year of life Electroencephalography and Clinical Neurophysiology, 61, 267-271

Sleep Patterns in Children of Superior Intelligence Journal of Child Psychology and Psychiatry, 24, 587-600

Evidence for a functional role for active (REM) sleep in infancy Sleep, 4, 185-191

Sleep duration and infant temperament   Journal of Pediatrics, 99, 817-819

Sleep and melatonin in infants   Sleep, 20, 185-191

Maternal entrainment of the developing circadian system Annals of the New York Academy of Science, 453, 162-169

Human wakefulness and biological rhythms after birth Archives of General Psychiatry, 32, 780-783

Other resources are cited in the text directly

About the Author, Tonya Sakowicz

Tonya is an INA Credentialed Nanny, Newborn Care Specialist, CAPPA trained Postpartum Doula and Parent Educator who does both consulting and in-home sleep conditioning and newborn care for her clients as well as the Owner and Director of Education for Newborn Care Solutions®, a company dedicated to the specialized training of high-level Newborn Care Specialists and the only company to offer the Master NCS® training program. Tonya attended Central Washington University, has over 36 years of experience as a Nanny and Newborn Care Specialist and is a proud wife and mother of two children. She is also a certified Eco-Maternity Consultant and Green Birth Educator through her partner company, Baby Go Green.

In addition to being credentialed through the International Nanny Association, Tonya served 2 years as Co-President of the organization and several years on both the executive and general board, is the past Chair of the Nanny to Nanny Mentoring Program and has served as the NCS Committee chair and in their Monday Mentor Program. Tonya is also the past Scottsdale Chapter President for DEMA, the Domestic Estate Management Association. Tonya is a highly in-demand speaker for the INA's annual conferences and has spoken at several National Association of Nannies conferences, as well as speaking for APNA, the Association of Premier Nanny Agencies at their annual conference. Tonya has spoken multiple times at National Nanny Training Days around the country and for nanny agencies nationwide. She is a founding member and serves on the advisory board for The Baby Dream Team, a group of dedicated Newborn Care Specialists who offer their services as volunteers to families around the country experiencing the birth of higher order multiples. She is a contributing 'expert' for the website NannyPro.com, has been published in and/or appeared in Parents Magazine, Child Magazine, The Seattle Times, The AZ Republic, The Wall Street Journal and the INAVision. Tonya has also made numerous television appearances including spots on the news in Seattle, Portland and Phoenix as well as an appearance in 2007 on the Today Show for a special on the Masche Miracles (a family with sextuplets).

Tonya was voted the **Professional Childcare Provider of the Year in 2003** and nominated for the **International Nanny Association Nanny of the Year** in 2004. In addition, that same year, she was deeply honored with a nomination by her peers for the National Association of **Nannies Harriette Grant Memorial Award**. In 2016, Tonya was honored with the **DEMA Educator of the Year Award** and most recently, in 2017, was again honored with the **DEMA Educator of the Year** and was the recipient of their prestigious **DEMA Lifetime Achievement Award**.

Along with her husband Todd, Tonya has founded Newborn Care Solutions, a company dedicated to education for families with newborns through the training of Newborn Care Specialists and for helping families adjust to life with their newborn baby.

In her spare time, Tonya likes to knit, cook, travel with her family and explore the world underneath the sea through scuba diving around the world.

Made in the USA
Las Vegas, NV
06 February 2024

85241762R00098